Who Was
Booker T. Washington?

by James Buckley Jr.

illustrated by Jake Murray

Penguin Workshop
An Imprint of Penguin Random House

This is for all students:
Use the story of Mr. Washington and
understand the power of education
to help you reach your goals!—JB

For Get Nichols, whose encouragement and
enthusiasm for education was invaluable to my
formative years and beyond—JM

PENGUIN WORKSHOP
Penguin Young Readers Group
An Imprint of Penguin Random House LLC

Text copyright © 2018 by James Buckley Jr. Illustrations copyright © 2018 by Penguin Random House LLC. All rights reserved. Published by Penguin Workshop, an imprint of Penguin Random House LLC, 345 Hudson Street, New York, New York 10014. PENGUIN and PENGUIN WORKSHOP are trademarks of Penguin Books Ltd. WHO HQ & Design is a registered trademark of Penguin Random House LLC. Printed in the USA.

Library of Congress Cataloging-in-Publication Data is available.

ISBN 9780448488516 (paperback)   10 9 8 7 6 5 4 3 2 1
ISBN 9781524786120 (library binding)   10 9 8 7 6 5 4 3 2 1

Contents

Who Was Booker T. Washington?

Booker T. Washington was born a slave in the Southern state of Virginia in 1856. He was one of millions of people of African descent forced to work in the fields of large farms, called plantations, without pay. They were considered property by white people who called themselves masters.

White children lived in and near the plantation, too. They were the sons and daughters of the masters and paid white workers. They studied together in a schoolhouse. As a young boy, Booker walked by the school building many times. He knew something amazing was happening inside, and he wanted very badly to be a part of it.

Sometimes, he would be told to carry the books of one of the plantation master's daughters. He would walk her to the door of the schoolhouse, but no farther. He peered inside before the door closed in his face.

He later wrote that "the picture of several dozen boys and girls engaged in study made a deep impression upon me, and I had the feeling that to get into a schoolhouse and study in this way would be about the same as getting into paradise."

Booker dreamed about the world of books, reading, and education. But it was a risky dream.

Enslaved children were not allowed to go to school. It was even illegal for a slave to learn to read! One of the main reasons white owners didn't want slaves to be educated was so that they would not find out about the world outside their plantation.

"From the moment that [I was told] that it was dangerous for me to learn to read . . . I resolved that I should never be satisfied until I learned what this dangerous practice was like." Booker knew that if he was caught with a book, he might be whipped as punishment.

But still he dreamed. And Booker made learning his life. He studied hard and eventually became a teacher. He helped thousands of African Americans and former slaves get an education.

He also inspired the creation of dozens of schools and universities for black people.

Booker worked his whole life to give others the chance at learning that he had struggled to get. His devotion to education for African Americans made him famous around the world. He showed that with focus and determination, a person could come "up from slavery" to a better life.

CHAPTER 1
A Difficult Beginning

When Booker T. Washington was born on a farm in Virginia on April 5, 1856, he did not have a last name. He was just called Booker. He was born a slave. Booker's mother, Jane, was also a slave. She cooked for everyone on the farm. Booker's older brother, John, was a slave, too. "Who my father was, I have never been able to learn with any degree of certainty," Booker wrote.

Dozens of other slaves lived and worked on the farm. They were forced to do whatever work their masters—the bosses on the farm—told them to do. They weren't paid for their labor. All the slaves were owned by Mr. Burroughs. They had no rights of their own.

The slaves on the Burroughs farm were not alone. Throughout the Southern United States, millions of black people were enslaved. For more than one hundred years, they had been kidnapped and taken from Africa to the United States and islands throughout the Caribbean. Slaves were considered property, the same as a horse for riding or a plow to use in the fields.

Families were broken up and sold to other plantations. Children could be taken from their mothers and sold, too. If a slave ever dared to disobey his master, he could be punished by whipping or worse.

About his early life as a slave, Booker later wrote that it "had its beginning in the midst of the most miserable, desolate, and discouraging surrounding."

Booker's home was a small shack. The floor was dirt and there were no windows—just the openings where windows should have been. The door was a thin plank of wood that did not shut completely. Cold wind blew in during the winter, and dust blew through in the summer. The children in Booker's family slept on a pile of rags on the floor.

The first pair of shoes Booker wore had soles made of wood and were very uncomfortable. His clothes were made from a rough and scratchy fabric called flax. Booker said that putting on his new flax shirt was "torture."

Jane was very busy cooking all day long and could not spend much time with her sons.

Booker later wrote that his family never sat down to a meal together. He said that the children got their meals "much as the dumb animals [got] theirs."

Most of the family's shack was taken up with the cooking fire and pots and pans, leaving only a tiny space for Jane and her children. The center of the floor was dug into a pit where potatoes were stored.

Booker worked in the fields and around his home, helping Jane. He had no winter clothes. When he was sick, his mother took care of him.

There were no doctors for slaves. In 1861, when Booker was about five, he was included on a list that showed the value of the Burroughs slaves as property. It read: "1 Negro Boy (Booker)—$400."

The life of a slave was one of constant work. The white people who owned slaves did not let their "property" learn to read or go to school, or even hope for a better future. The plantation masters saw no value in educating slaves. But not everyone in America believed that owning slaves was right.

The Civil War, which began in 1861, was fought for several reasons, but the biggest was slavery. Most Northern states were against slavery. Most Southern states were for it. The Southern plantations relied on slaves to do the difficult field work for free. That meant more profit for the landowners. Many Southerners believed that black people were simply not human.

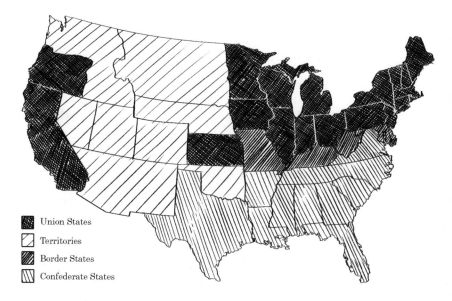

Union States

Territories

Border States

Confederate States

The Southern states did not want to be told what to do by Northern states that did not rely on farming as much.

As Civil War battles raged throughout the South and even into some Northern states, President Abraham Lincoln issued the Emancipation Proclamation.

The Emancipation Proclamation

In 1808, a United States law went into effect that banned bringing slaves into the country. But states in the South continued the practice of slavery with the descendants of their African slaves for more than a half century. Many in the North argued strongly against the ongoing enslavement, but could do little about it.

Finally, on September 22, 1862, President Abraham Lincoln, who was strongly against slavery, wanted to make his beliefs clear. He wrote a document called the Emancipation Proclamation. (*Emancipation* means freedom.) In it, he proclaimed that, as of January 1, 1863, all slaves in Southern states "shall be then, thenceforward, and forever free." It was a bold statement and the first time that a US president had written a formal anti-slavery statement. It was not a law, but it was an inspiring event.

It wasn't until after the Civil War ended in 1865 that the United States added the Thirteenth Amendment to the US Constitution. It said that "All persons are equal before the law, so that no person can hold another as a slave."

The Emancipation Proclamation paved the way for equality to become law.

For two years after President Lincoln's proclamation, the war continued. Booker, along with nearly four million other people, remained enslaved. The Civil War became the deadliest in the nation's history.

More than 620,000 American soldiers were killed. In April 1865, the Union Army of the North won the Civil War. Lincoln's proclamation could now be enforced in the South.

Booker remembered the day a Union Army
officer visited the Burroughs farm. The officer
gathered the slaves together and read the
Proclamation. Jane, Booker, and their family
realized with amazement that they were no
longer slaves.

"There was great rejoicing, and thanksgiving," Booker later wrote. At the time, he was nine years old. And he was free.

CHAPTER 2
New Opportunities

Once she was free, Jane took her family away from the Burroughs farm as soon as she could.

They headed to Malden, West Virginia, to join Washington Ferguson, Jane's husband. Now Jane, Booker, and John could finally live together as a family. Jane and Washington already had a daughter named Amanda, and they soon adopted another son—an orphan named James. They had a small house in Malden. It was not fancy, but it was much nicer than their slave shack had been.

Washington had been working in a Virginia coal mine. Once the family arrived in Malden, he took his stepsons with him to the mine.

It was hard and dangerous work. And Booker did not like it. He said, "I do not believe that one ever experiences anywhere else such darkness as he does in a coal-mine."

Washington sometimes also worked in a salt works—a type of factory that boiled water to get the salt out of it. Once the water was removed, the salt had to be shoveled into huge barrels. John and Booker joined their stepfather in the difficult and dirty work of packing the barrels. When they were done, a manager put the number "18" on each one, which was Washington's worker ID number. And that was the first number Booker ever remembered learning.

Booker knew that a life in the coal mine or the salt works was not right for him. He remembered the schoolhouse from the Burroughs farm and

William Davis

knew that he wanted to have an education. Jane got him an alphabet book to learn his letters, but he wanted more. Not long after they arrived in Malden, a teacher named William Davis helped set up a small school for black children.

When he was nine, Booker was one of the first people to attend the school. He was grateful for the opportunity to learn. But his stepfather wanted to put a stop to it. Washington wanted Booker to keep working to help the family. Jane came up with a plan.

Booker would work in the salt works from 4:00 to 9:00 a.m., then go to school. After school, he could return to work if they needed him at the salt works. It would take a lot of effort, but for Booker, it was worth it.

To make sure he got to school on time, Booker even changed the clocks at the salt works. He set them back so that they were a half hour early.

That way, he could work until "nine" and still get to school on time! The trick didn't last long, but it showed how much he wanted to be at school on time.

Soon after he began school, Booker finally got a last name. Mr. Davis asked what Booker's father's name was, and the young man said, "Washington," giving his *first* name. The teacher wrote that down and the new student was called Booker Washington from then on. (Later in life, Booker gave himself a middle name, Taliaferro.)

Booker T. Washington

When Booker was eleven, Jane convinced Viola Ruffner, who was white and the wife of the owner of the salt mine, to hire Booker to work as one of her houseboys. Booker was smart and Jane had taught him to be clean and neat. He soon was given a room in the Ruffner house.

Mrs. Ruffner slowly gave Booker more and more to do. He learned to clean the house and to keep track of the fruit and vegetables that she

sold to her neighbors. Doing his chores improved his math skills. Mrs. Ruffner had been a teacher, so she added her own lessons to the ones Booker got at school. "He was always willing to quit play for study and he was more than willing to follow directions," she later wrote.

One of the most important things Mrs. Ruffner taught Booker was how to speak more clearly so that he could be understood. Many ex-slaves spoke in slang with a Southern accent that some white people had a hard time understanding. Mrs. Ruffner helped Booker to become confident enough to speak well in public.

In addition to his job for Mrs. Ruffner, Booker sometimes worked in the coal mine to earn extra money. One day in the mine he heard some of the men talking about the Hampton Institute—a school in Virginia for poor black students. Booker wanted to make every effort to continue his studies, and he thought the Hampton Institute might be just the place for him.

CHAPTER 3
A Home at Hampton

In September 1872, Booker left Malden and headed for the Hampton Institute. He gathered up whatever money he could find and set off for the school, even though he had "no definite idea where Hampton was."

It turned out to be five hundred miles from his home to the school in Virginia! Booker only had enough money to go part of the way by train. He took the next part of his journey by stagecoach, and then he began walking. He sometimes hitched rides in passing buggies. He stopped along the

way at an inn where the owner would not let him inside because he was black. Booker knew that although slavery had ended, black people were treated as unfairly as ever. He stayed outside in the cold until the next morning when another stagecoach arrived.

After weeks on the road, he reached Richmond, Virginia. He was out of money and still had not reached his goal, which was almost a hundred miles away. Booker was determined, though, and found a solution. He slept outside and then found work to earn enough money to continue his journey.

Booker arrived at Hampton tired, hungry, and dirty. He was asked to clean one of the classrooms as a test to see if he was a hard worker. Because Booker had plenty of experience cleaning for Mrs. Ruffner, he did a great job in the classroom.

The school welcomed him as a student. He got a job as a janitor to help pay for his schooling. Booker was overjoyed. He wrote later that he believed that a "new kind of existence had now begun . . . Life would now have a new meaning."

Since he had never had a real bed, he didn't know what to do with the sheets the school gave him. It took him two nights before he figured out how to put them on the mattress!

While at Hampton, Booker studied math and composition (writing). He also spent time working on the school's farm, helping take care of the pigs. He studied biology and learned about animals and plants. But he loved his classes in public speaking the most.

The leader of the Hampton Institute was a white former Union Army general named Samuel Chapman Armstrong who had led black troops during the Civil War. General Armstrong was the founder of the Hampton Institute. He was a huge influence on Booker, who later called him "more than a father." Booker also wrote that "there

General Samuel Chapman Armstrong

was something about [Armstrong] that was superhuman."

General Armstrong believed strongly that black people should have a practical education. He thought they should learn how to do skilled jobs with their hands, like farming, carpentry, and bricklaying. Though Booker and students at Hampton took classes in writing, math, and science, they spent most of their time learning specific trades and skills. All the teachers at that time were white.

Hampton Institute

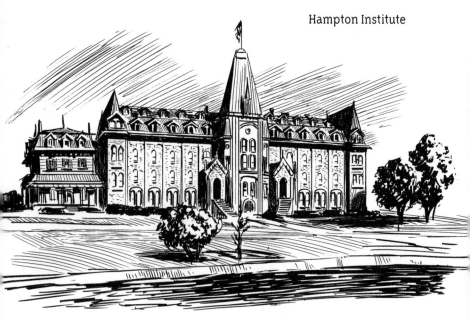

The organization of the school was similar to daily army life. All students had to get up at five o'clock in the morning and clean up for inspection. Breakfast and morning prayers were followed by classwork until three. Students then worked around the school or marched in drills until dinner. Then it was time for more schoolwork, prayers, and bed at about 9:30 p.m.

Samuel Chapman Armstrong (1839–1893)

Samuel Armstrong was born in Hawaii. His father had been a missionary there. After fighting at the Battle of Gettysburg on the side of the Union Army, he was given command of a Civil War regiment of African Americans. They were called "Colored Troops" at that time. General Armstrong led the troops until the end of the war.

Inspired by the missionary work he had grown up with, he wanted to educate his soldiers as well as lead them. When the war was over, Armstrong continued his dream and—with the help of the American Missionary Association—established the Hampton Institute in 1868. He wanted to train black leaders to help other black people. While inspiring Booker T. Washington and many others, Armstrong ran Hampton until his death in 1893.

Some black leaders felt that the school was not doing enough to teach the students more advanced subjects. Unlike white schools, Hampton did not teach Latin or Greek or philosophy or complicated sciences. White university students arrived at their schools with much more knowledge than Armstrong's students. The Hampton Institute began with simple and basic lessons.

Some of those lessons taught students how to take care of themselves. Hampton stressed keeping clean and always looking nice. For his part, Booker took one of these lessons very seriously.

"I have watched carefully the influence of the toothbrush and I am convinced that there are few [things] in civilization that are more far-reaching."

Booker's time at Hampton had a huge influence on his life. He wrote that it "caused me for the first time to realize what it meant to be a man instead of a piece of property."

In 1874, Booker returned to Malden for a summer break. To help pay for another year at Hampton, he worked in the coal mines and even back at Mrs. Ruffner's house. While Booker was home, his mother, who had been ill for some time, died. Though he was greatly saddened, Booker knew that he had to continue his education, and he returned to Hampton.

Booker graduated from the Hampton Institute with honors in 1875. He was nineteen years old and had come a long way from the coal mines and slavery. He spoke in front of his classmates as part of the graduation ceremonies. A reporter from the *New York Times* attended the event and singled out Booker as the student "who distinguished himself most."

CHAPTER 4
The Teacher Teaches

With his degree from Hampton, it was time for Booker to put his education to work. And he was lucky enough to do that in a familiar place. In the summer of 1875, he returned to the town of Malden to run the Tinkersville neighborhood school.

One of his students was his own brother, John! Booker would later help pay for John to attend Hampton, too.

Booker did all he could to educate his students in Malden.

John Washington

He added a night school so that students who worked during the day could still come to class. He taught Sunday school for his church, including one session at the salt factory where he used to work. He created a library for black residents, and he always had newspapers and magazines available for everyone to read. He wanted to spread the lessons he had learned at Hampton

about education and self-improvement to anyone who was willing to learn.

He also made sure his Tinkersville students stayed as neat as he had been at Hampton. "I require all [my students] to keep their clothes neat and clean and their hair combed every morning and the boys to keep their boots cleaned," he wrote to a friend at Hampton.

Booker believed so much in the importance
of being able to express his ideas that he started
a debating club in Malden. He invited the
community to come and discuss popular and

important issues. Malden challenged nearby towns to debating contests, which Booker often helped them win. He also worked as a clerk for the local African Zion Baptist Church.

In 1878, Booker decided to attended the Wayland Seminary School in Washington, DC. The Wayland School trained ministers and preachers. Booker was a Christian who had always had very strong faith.

But he did not stay long. Booker missed the hard work and the routine he had at Hampton and in Malden. He worried that the way that the future ministers were being taught would not work in the real world.

"They knew more about Latin and Greek when they left the school, but they seemed to know less about life and its conditions as they would meet it at their homes." Booker believed what he had learned at Hampton: that black people needed to learn lessons that would help them succeed in their daily life.

While he was in Washington, Booker did get to hear the famous African American leader Frederick Douglass speak.

Frederick Douglass (1818–1895)

Although Frederick Douglass was born a slave, he still managed to learn to read. In 1838, he escaped slavery in Maryland and moved north to Massachusetts and later New York. He continued his education and began to speak out about life as a slave.

His skill at writing and giving speeches amazed the many people who came to hear him speak. He published a popular autobiography in 1845. Some whites believed that a black person could not have written such a great book.

Frederick Douglass became the most important African American in the country in the decades before the Civil War. He spoke out against slavery, and he was in favor of women's rights. He believed in the equality of all people. During the war, Douglass advised President Abraham Lincoln about the issue of slavery.

Following the war, Douglass was one of the first black people to hold office in the US government. He was appointed consul general to the Dominican Republic and to Haiti in 1889.

In 1879, General Armstrong asked Booker to speak at the Hampton graduation. Booker gave a speech he called "The Force that Wins." It summed up all the beliefs he had on the importance of going to school and making the right choices. He told the graduates that the "force that wins" called for more than books. Students needed to have "wisdom and common sense, a heart set on the right and a trust in God."

General Armstrong was very impressed with the speech. He asked Booker to return to Hampton, this time as a teacher. He put Booker in charge of a group of poor students who had to take night classes after working all day to earn their school fees. Booker did his job so well that these students soon joined the regular students. This group was known as the "Plucky Class," for their spirit and hard work. It became a badge of honor to be made part of this group of students who worked so hard at both their studies and jobs.

Booker taught public speaking, English, geography, and personal health care at the Hampton Institute for two years. And then, with a recommendation from General Armstrong, he began an entirely new chapter in his life.

CHAPTER 5
Mr. Washington's New Job

In 1881, the state of Alabama created a new school to educate black people to become teachers. It was called the Tuskegee Normal School. At the time, "Normal" meant a school for training teachers. The organizers of the school wrote to General Armstrong to see if he could recommend a white teacher to lead the school. Instead, Armstrong suggested Booker.

The Hampton Institute leader called his former student "clear headed, modest, sensible, polite, and a thorough teacher and superior man. The best man we ever had here."

And so the state of Alabama chose Booker.

Booker would be missed at Hampton. His Plucky Class students gave him a watch chain

to say thank you for all he had done for them. After stopping to see his family in Malden, Booker headed to Tuskegee, a city in central Alabama about 180 miles north of the Gulf of Mexico.

When Booker arrived at his new "school" in June 1881, all he found was an empty lot. There was money to start setting up the school, but no buildings, no students, and no teachers. Booker would have to do it all.

He found a local church that lent him a spare room to teach in. He advertised in the local paper to find students. And he hired a teacher to help him. On July 4, Booker welcomed the first thirty students to Tuskegee Normal School.

It was not exactly a perfect beginning. Booker later wrote that the roof leaked so much that a student held an umbrella over him as he read to the class.

Even though he had already started teaching classes, Booker also had to begin the hard work of building the school itself. He spoke often to groups of local white businessmen to raise money. He believed that they would support a school that would help black people learn new skills. By educating workers who could then earn more money, Booker was creating customers for their stores.

Booker also got a loan from General J. F. B. Marshall, one of General Armstrong's assistants at Hampton. Others at Hampton sent classroom materials like maps, books, and globes. Soon Booker had enough money to buy one hundred acres of farmland just outside the town. Booker taught classes in the henhouse and in the stable. He used the farm's fields to grow sweet potatoes and other vegetables to feed students and to help pay for more school supplies.

Tuskegee Normal School

By November, the school had more than eighty students, and Booker hired more teachers to help him. One was Olivia Davidson, another

Hampton graduate. She soon became his top assistant and the Lady Principal in charge of female students at Tuskegee. She also came up with many ideas to raise money for the school from local

Olivia Davidson

black families and also from white Northerners.

By the summer of 1882, the school had paid off its loans and Booker had become a respected person in the community. He started what became regular trips to the Northern states to try to raise money for Tuskegee. He visited white families who believed that educating black people was the right thing to do. They felt that former slaves and their families deserved a chance at a better life. Booker's experience of working with white people like Mrs. Ruffner and General Armstrong helped him have great success on these tours.

Also that summer, he married Fannie Norton Smith. Fannie had been a former student of his at the Tinkersville school who had gone on to study at Hampton. They were married in Malden's African

Fannie Norton Smith

Zion Baptist Church and then returned together to Tuskegee.

In the years that followed, the number of students at the Alabama school grew too large for the small farm buildings. In order to expand, Booker would need the students' help. He hired experts to teach his students how to create every part of a new building.

For their new chapel, Booker's students cut the wood at the school's sawmill and formed

bricks by hand. (He hired his brother John as one of the leaders of the sawmill operation.)

Other students worked with architecture teachers to design the buildings. Still others made the furniture for classrooms. By doing this, the students not only created a new place to study, but they also learned valuable skills for the future.

In 1883, Booker and Fannie had a daughter named Portia. Sadly, Fannie died the very next year after falling from a wagon. Olivia Davidson became Booker's second wife in 1885, while continuing her work as Lady Principal at Tuskegee.

They had two sons, Baker and Ernest. (When he grew up, Baker changed his name to Booker Jr. after his father.) But tragedy struck again in 1889, just two days after Ernest was born. The smoke from a house fire damaged Olivia's lungs, and she died shortly after.

Even during these sad times, Booker continued to lead Tuskegee upward and outward. By the late 1880s, Booker was teaching less and fundraising more. He only spoke to the students during weekly chapel meetings.

In 1892, he married for a third time. Margaret Murray had come to the school to replace Olivia as Lady Principal, and she and Booker had quickly bonded.

As Booker continued to build Tuskegee, he was training his students to be teachers who have the "proper training of head, hand, and heart." He wanted his students to "lift themselves up" from the years of slavery their parents and grandparents had endured.

CHAPTER 6
The Atlanta Speech

By 1895, the Tuskegee Normal School had grown to more than one thousand students

studying in more than a dozen buildings on 1,800 acres of land! It was one of the largest schools in the American South. Booker had become nationally famous. He continued to speak out on the issues affecting black people, many of whom were trying to overcome the hardships and terrors of slavery.

On September 18, 1895, he was invited to speak at the Cotton States and International Exposition, a large gathering of white Southern farmers and businesspeople.

At the meeting in Atlanta, Georgia, Booker gave a short talk about his experiences and ideas. Booker spoke of his belief that the way forward for black Americans was not to seek instant equality with white Americans, but to seek a more gradual path. He believed that black people should work harder to move beyond the days of slavery.

Booker called for patience from black people and support from the white community. He didn't think that black people should quickly strive to all become businessmen or politicians. He felt they should focus on work with their hands in "agriculture, mechanics . . . or domestic service." This meant taking paying jobs as maids or farmers, the same work many slaves had done for free.

"No race can prosper till it learns that there is as much dignity in tilling a field as in writing a poem," he added.

Perhaps the most famous words from the speech were these: "In all things that are purely social, we can be as separate as the fingers, yet one as the hand in all things essential to mutual progress." He meant that in everyday life, black and white people could be separate, but they should come together in business and work.

This was what Southern white listeners wanted to hear.

They wanted to keep blacks separate from their lives, even as they continued to benefit from their work. In fact, Southern states had passed many laws making it legal to keep the races separate. Black and white children could not go to school together.

Black people could not use public libraries or attend public events with white people. Though the Civil War had freed slaves, it had not changed the beliefs or practices of many Southern whites.

Even some white leaders from the North praised the speech. President Grover Cleveland, who later visited the Exposition, spoke highly of Booker's ideas. Some black leaders praised the speech, too. "The speech by Professor Washington . . . was a magnificent effort and places him in the forefront of the representatives of our race," said an article in the *Richmond Planet* newspaper.

To a growing number of black people, however, the path forward suggested by Booker was too slow. They wanted equal rights, as granted to them by the US Constitution. And they wanted them now. Former slaves and the families of former slaves did not feel that they had to prove they were worthy. They didn't like the laws that kept blacks and whites separate. "He said something that was death to the Afro-American and elevating to the white people,"

W. Calvin Chase

wrote black newspaper editor W. Calvin Chase.

Privately, Booker tried to help the black cause in other ways. In Alabama, many court cases were brought by black citizens to try to get their legal rights. Booker sometimes paid lawyers or court fees for these citizens. But he never used his real name when he did so. Booker feared that if white people knew that he was helping blacks this way, they might stop supporting Tuskegee Institute.

The continued hatred of black people by whites was well known, even at Tuskegee. At the 1896 graduation ceremonies, Alabama governor William Oates became angry at some of the speeches, which called for more equal treatment. When it was his turn to speak, he ranted,

"You had better not listen to such speeches. You might as well understand this is a white man's country . . . and we are going to make you keep your place."

The US Supreme Court made this idea a law that very same year. The court said that "separate but equal" public places were legal. That gave Southern states legal approval to keep white and black citizens separate.

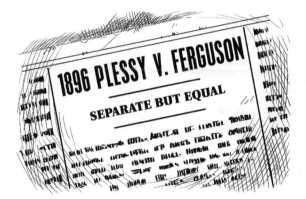

1896 PLESSY V. FERGUSON

SEPARATE BUT EQUAL

The decision hurt the cause of black equality.

Booker continued to help Tuskegee Institute grow. And his efforts to educate black people continued to be admired. In the fall of 1896,

he became the first African American to get an honorary degree from Harvard University in Cambridge, Massachusetts.

President William McKinley personally visited the Tuskegee campus in 1898. The Alabama state legislature attended the ceremony. The students demonstrated what they were growing and making for their important visitors. President McKinley praised the school. His approval helped Booker raise even more money for the Institute.

In 1899, Booker's friends encouraged him to take the longest vacation of his life. They arranged a trip to Europe for Booker and Margaret. He used his time away to get a lot of rest (at one point he slept for an entire day and a half!) but he also met some very important people. He told his story and the story of Tuskegee Institute in America.

The couple traveled to Paris, Belgium, England, and the Netherlands. When they were in London, they met former President Benjamin Harrison and famous American author Mark Twain. And England's Queen Victoria invited the couple to tea. The former slave who loved to read had come a very long way.

CHAPTER 7
Two Ways to Move Ahead

Booker wrote many letters, speeches, and magazine articles. In 1901, he published his most successful book. *Up from Slavery* gave many details about his difficult early life and about his steady rise in the world. He wrote about his ideals of hard work, education, and self-reliance. The book was very successful among both white and black readers. Within a couple of years, it had been translated into more than a dozen languages, including Braille.

Later that same year, Booker received a special honor. On October 16, 1901, Booker became the first black person to eat dinner at the White House as a guest of the president. When Theodore Roosevelt was still vice president, he had met Booker. And soon after becoming president, Roosevelt invited Booker to dinner.

News of the event was a sensation. Black people all over the country were thrilled. It was a signal to them that they were making progress. A leader from their own community was going to meet with the nation's leader for a meal at the White House!

But white people in the South were not happy about it. To them, having a black person over to your home for dinner was unthinkable. And

to have a black person invited to the White House—the nation's house—was shocking. A newspaper in Tennessee called the event a terrible "outrage."

But the dinner was a sign that white leaders agreed with Booker. His idea that it was okay to keep people separated based on their race was welcomed by whites and some blacks. In fact, for the next several years, President Roosevelt took Booker's advice many times on black-white relations.

The president's Republican party made campaign buttons in 1904 showing Booker and the president eating together above the word "Equality."

Some black leaders continued to disagree with Booker's views on how to best help his people. One such person was W. E. B. Du Bois. In 1895, Du Bois had praised Booker's Atlanta speech. Over time, though, Du Bois changed his mind. In 1903, he published a book of essays called *The Souls of Black Folk*. In it, he criticized Booker's "submission and silence to civil and political rights." Du Bois later labeled Booker's speech

"The Atlanta Compromise." He did not think the black population of America should have to prove their worth by compromising and accepting the "separate but equal" law.

W. E. B. Du Bois was not alone in his criticism of Booker. William Trotter was the editor of a black newspaper in Boston. Trotter called Booker "The Great Traitor." Many others began to feel the same way.

William Trotter

Like other black people living in the Northern United States, Du Bois had a very different experience from those living in the South. He and his family and other Northern blacks had never been slaves. They felt that equality should be granted to them immediately. When Booker said that "separate" was okay, these people disagreed.

Booker wrote that young black people had to work twice as hard as white people to get ahead in the world. He believed that the struggle and extra work would make them appreciate what they had. But others believed that it was not right that black people had that struggle in the first place.

Most white Northerners, as well as some Southerners, agreed that blacks should have equal rights. Whether black Americans should wait patiently to become equal was a debate that continued for decades.

W. E. B. Du Bois (1868–1963)

For more than seventy years, William Edward Burghardt "W. E. B." Du Bois was an important African American thinker, writer, and leader. He grew up a free man in Massachusetts and never knew the horrors of slavery. He studied at Fisk University and Harvard University and was later a professor at Wilberforce University and Atlanta University.

In his writings, he called for full equality for all African Americans. Du Bois wrote *The Souls of Black Folk* in 1903, which encouraged more aggressive moves toward black equality. He became the leading voice against Booker T. Washington's plans and ideas.

Du Bois helped found the National Association for the Advancement of Colored People (NAACP) in 1909 and was the editor of the association's journal *The Crisis*. At the age of ninety-three he moved to the African nation of Ghana, where he died in 1963, just one short year before the United States enacted the Civil Rights Act. The act outlawed discrimination based on race, color, religion, sex, or national origin.

CHAPTER 8
Finishing the Work

In 1905, President Roosevelt visited Booker at Tuskegee Institute. Together they watched the parade of floats and wagons that had been decorated by the students. A bed of flowers spelled out the president's name. Both men gave speeches praising the other. Roosevelt's visit brought national attention to the school at a time when Booker was being criticized by other black leaders for thinking that "slow but steady" equality was a good plan.

The very next year, rumors spread in Atlanta that some black men had attacked a group of white women. Whether this was true or not, a white mob formed. They wanted to get revenge. In September 1906, they attacked black people in the streets. The mob rampaged for days until enough police arrived to stop them. As many as thirty black people had been killed in the fighting.

Black leaders spoke out loudly against the riots. Booker asked people to be careful. He wanted black people to remain calm. But the Atlanta incident wasn't the only case of black outrage.

Earlier in the summer, some US Army soldiers in Brownsville, Texas, were charged with taking part in a murder. All of the accused soldiers were black.

The case was never proven, but the people of Texas demanded action. And since the soldiers were US troops, the decision was up to President Roosevelt.

In October of 1906, Booker visited the president to urge him to help calm things down. Instead, Roosevelt told Booker he wanted to fire all the black soldiers who had been accused of the Texas murder. Booker was shocked and hurt by Roosevelt's decision.

When President William Taft won the next election in early November, he fired the soldiers. But it was Theodore Roosevelt who took the blame among black people. And since Booker had a close relationship with Roosevelt, he was blamed, too. It was becoming harder and harder for people to listen to Booker's ideas about slow and steady change. The outcry for equality was growing.

In 1909, Du Bois, with help from both black and white supporters, founded the National Association for the Advancement of Colored People. The group soon became the national voice for black Americans, much as Booker had been for many years.

Though his influence was fading, Booker kept working. He was over fifty years old, but he still believed strongly in his plan. In 1900, he had helped create the National Negro Business League, formed to help black people open new companies or make existing businesses stronger.

For the next decade, Booker also worked tirelessly to raise money to support Tuskegee Institute. Most years, he spent more than half his time away from the school, making speech after speech and visiting donors. All of his traveling took a toll on Booker's health. As he grew weaker, he developed diabetes and heart problems. His family and friends tried to get him to slow down but—as always—Booker wanted to keep working.

CHAPTER 9
A Legacy of Learning

After founding the National Negro Business League, Booker's health continued to worsen. During a trip to New York in 1915, he became very sick. Doctors there told him that he might not have much more time to live. Booker's wife Margaret traveled from Alabama to take him home.

On November 14, 1915, Booker T. Washington died from kidney failure in his bed at Tuskegee Institute, the place he loved best. Millions of people, both black and white, mourned his death. He was praised around the country for the many great things he had done for African Americans.

After Booker's death, Robert Moton took over as the leader of Tuskegee for the next twenty years. Dr. Moton was succeeded in 1935 by Dr. Frederick D. Patterson. It was Dr. Patterson who brought the Tuskegee Airmen flight training program to the Institute.

The school Booker had founded grew steadily and remains an important center of learning for African Americans. Over the years, Tuskegee moved away from Booker's focus on developing technical and farming skills toward more traditional college classes. It became a full university in 1985. Today, it has more than 3,100 students and has produced thousands of black scientists, educators, engineers, and military officers.

The Tuskegee Airmen

The Tuskegee Airmen were the first African American military pilots in the US Armed Forces. During World War II (1939–1945), many US states and the American military were still racially segregated.

All of the black fighter and bomber pilots who trained in the United States trained at Moton Field, the Tuskegee Army Air Field, and were educated at Tuskegee University. Officially, the Tuskegee Airmen made up the 332nd Fighter Group and the 477th Bombardment Group of the US Army Air Forces.

Perhaps Booker's longest lasting legacy is in schools like Tuskegee University. There are now more than a hundred colleges and universities that have been established to help African American students. Among the most important are Howard University, Spelman College, Morehouse College, and Grambling University. The school Booker attended under the guidance of General Armstrong is now called Hampton University. The largest such school is Florida A&M University, with nearly ten thousand students.

Monument to Booker T. Washington at Hampton University

During the years after Booker's death, dozens of laws continued to keep blacks and whites separate in the American South. These laws, called "Jim Crow" laws, had started in the late 1800s and early 1900s. They continued to create separate schools, swimming pools, drinking fountains, trains, restaurants, and more. In the North and West, segregation was not the law, but black citizens still struggled with widespread racism in many forms.

In the years after World War II, a growing civil rights movement began in the South and spread around the country. Booker's way of thinking was no longer embraced by African Americans. When he wrote, "The race cannot expect to get everything at once. It must learn to wait and bide its time," Booker could probably not imagine the movements of the 1950s and '60s. Modern civil rights protesters called for fast change, new laws, and equal rights.

They were rejecting the slow pace of change.
They wanted action . . . now.

The Civil Rights Act of 1964 put an end to legalized discrimination and segregation. Equality between white Americans and African Americans is now the law. But although the US elected its first black president, Barack Obama, in 2008, the struggle for equal treatment for all people continues today.

Booker T. Washington was born a slave and became the leading voice of former slaves and their descendants. He was a black American leader who believed in education and business opportunities for all African Americans.

He worked constantly to change the lives of people like himself, people who came "up from slavery" looking for a better life.

Timeline of Booker T. Washington's Life

1856	Booker T. Washington is born a slave, known simply as "Booker" without a last name, on a plantation in Hale's Ford, Virginia
1865	Freed along with other slaves after the Civil War ends Moves to Malden, West Virginia
1872	Arrives at the Hampton Institute, graduating in 1875
1879	Returns to Hampton Institute as a teacher
1881	Opens Tuskegee Normal School in Tuskegee, Alabama
1882	Marries Fannie Norton Smith
1883	Daughter Portia born
1885	After death of Fannie a year earlier, marries Olivia Davidson
1887	Son Baker (later Booker T. Jr.) born
1889	Son Ernest born; wife Olivia dies
1892	Marries Margaret Murray
1895	Delivers important speech at the Cotton States and International Exposition in Atlanta
1896	Receives honorary degree from Harvard University
1899	Travels with Margaret to Europe
1900	Founds National Negro Business League
1901	Publishes autobiography, *Up from Slavery* Dines at White House with President Theodore Roosevelt
1915	Dies at Tuskegee Institute at age of fifty-nine

Timeline of the World

1848	California Gold Rush begins
1852	Napoleon III declared emperor of France
1861	American Civil War begins; it ends in 1865
1871	Bavaria and Prussia unify to create modern Germany
1872	The US Congress names Yellowstone the world's first national park
1880	Thomas Alva Edison patents the first working lightbulb
1887	A flood on the Yellow River in China kills 900,000 people
1893	New Zealand becomes the first country to give women the vote in national elections
1896	The first modern Olympic Games are held in Athens, Greece
1901	Guglielmo Marconi sends first radio signals across the Atlantic Ocean
1903	The Wright brothers fly the first airplane
1907	An earthquake in Kingston, Jamaica, kills one thousand people
1910	William Howard Taft is the first US president to throw out the first ball at a baseball game on April 15
1914	World War I begins
1915	Pluto is photographed for the first time on March 19

Bibliography

* Books for young readers

* Asim, Jabari. *Fifty Cents and a Dream: Young Booker T. Washington*.
New York: Little, Brown for Young Readers, 2012.

* Braun, Eric. *Booker T. Washington: Great American Educator*.
Minneapolis: Capstone Press, 2006.

Harlan, Louis R. *Booker T. Washington: The Making of a Black Leader,
1856–1901*. New York: Oxford University Press, 1972.

Norrell, Robert J. *Up from History: The Life of Booker T. Washington*.
Cambridge, MA: Belknap Press, 2009.

Sanneh, Kelefa. "The Wizard." *The New Yorker*, February 2, 2009.

Washington, Booker T. *An Autobiography: The Story of My Life and
Work*. 1900. Reprint, CreateSpace Independent Publishing Platform,
2012.

Washington, Booker T. "The Awakening of the Negro." *The Atlantic*,
September 1896.

Washington, Booker T. *Up from Slavery*. 1901. Reprint, Mineola, NY:
Dover, 1996.

Websites

Booker T. Washington, "Atlanta Compromise" (speech) Atlanta Exposition,
September 18, 1895. www.history.com/topics/black-history/booker-t-
washington/speeches.